SECRETS IN A DEAD FISH

The Spying Game in the
First World War

MELANIE KING

Bodleian Library
UNIVERSITY OF OXFORD

First published in 2014 by the Bodleian Library
Broad Street
Oxford OX1 3BG

www.bodleianbookshop.co.uk

ISBN 978 1 85124 260 3

Text © Melanie King
All images © Bodleian Library, University of Oxford, 2014

Every effort has been made to obtain permission to use material which is in copyright. The publisher would welcome any omissions being brought to their attention.

Cover design by Dot Little
Illustrations by Bernard Chau
Designed and typeset in 11 on 14 point Dante
by illuminati, Grosmont
Printed and bound by C&C Joint Printing Ltd., Hong Kong
on 100 gsm Shenbom Lawrence paper

British Library Catalogue in Publishing Data
A CIP record of this publication is available
from the British Library

Contents

Introduction

IN THE DECADES following the Great War, memoirs, diaries and personal accounts of the conflict rolled steadily off the presses in both Europe and America. Readers could learn about the war in all its brutal manifestations, choosing from accounts by cavalrymen, infantrymen, chaplains, naval captains, nurses, US Marines, and enlisted soldiers of every background. In London in the year 1922 alone at least ten separate memoirs appeared, including Aubrey Smith's *Four Years on the Western Front* and H. Drummond Gauld's *The Truth from the Trenches*. The latter described in unsparing detail the experiences of an artilleryman at the Battle of the Somme.

It is no surprise that members of the secret intelligence services should also have offered their recollections to an international readership eager to learn of the exploits of those who served in the Great War. Perhaps the first of these memoirs to appear was the US Marine and former circus clown Courtney Ryley Cooper's *The Eagle's Eye*. Purporting to tell the true story of German spies operating in America during the war, it was first published in January 1919. Hot on its heels came Camillo de Carlo's *The Flying Spy*, published in Italian in 1919 and available to American readers in an English translation by August of that same year.

Former spies and intelligence agents were required to tread carefully, however. Unlike other memoirists, they needed to be judiciously sparing in their details. It was necessary for them to inform and excite their readers without angering the intelligence services for whom they worked or, worse still, endangering the lives of their fellow agents and informers. In 1932, one of the most famous memoirs of Great War espionage, Compton Mackenzie's *Greek Memories*, was banned from publication. Mackenzie, the future author of *Whisky Galore*, was prosecuted at the Old Bailey under the Official Secrets Act for having revealed the identity of 'C' – the head of the Secret Intelligence Service – as Sir Manfield Cumming, and for divulging that the Foreign Office's passport control departments were nests of spies. An expurgated version of Mackenzie's book was published in 1939, and not until 2011 was it issued in a full and unabridged edition.

The Bodleian Library holds one of the original 1932 copies of Mackenzie's *Greek Memories*, shelved for many years in its 'suppressed books' section. The Bodleian also holds numerous other memoirs of Great War spies, including ones by British, German, American and Russian agents. One of them, Nicholas Everitt, an agent for British Naval Intelligence in Scandinavia, tried to allay fears that by publishing *The British Secret Service during the Great War* he might be giving away dangerous secrets and compromising state security. 'I can assure my reader', he wrote in his preface, 'that nothing has been divulged which touched even the fringe of the important secrets that every Secret Service agent would personally guard with his life.'[1] The authorities were not entirely convinced. When Everitt departed for a speaking and publicity tour of the United States in 1920, the Secret Intelligence Service took the precaution of discrediting him, with the head of station in New York boasting that he had 'cramped his style' by planting ridiculous stories about him in American newspapers. It was a classic disinformation campaign that the spy in Everitt may have been able to appreciate.[2]

Another of the spy memoirs, Captain Ferdinand Tuohy's *The Secret Corps: A Tale of 'Intelligence' on All Fronts*, came with a similar disclaimer. It left the author in the awkward position of having to confess that he had been forced for reasons of security to make omissions. 'What may be termed the "acid test of secrecy" has been applied to this narrative', he wrote in a preface dated March 1920. 'How many secrets it may unfold to the general reader is irrelevant. The test is: Does anything figure in this book that is not already known to the General Staffs of our late allies and enemies alike, or that would come as valuable information to such staffs? Intelligence officers, possibly the best judges in the matter, will appreciate that in order faithfully to subscribe to such test it has been necessary to omit almost as much about Intelligence work as is here set down in type.'[3]

Captain Tuohy no doubt protested too much. His memoir, like Everitt's, is certainly filled with fascinating details about espionage that, as he noted, would have unfolded secrets to the man in the street, if not to members of the intelligence services. But his comment about the need for omissions recalls Sir Mansfield Cumming's jocular comment that his own memoir of being a spymaster would have 'four hundred pages, all blank'.[4]

The potential dangers of divulging too many secrets is illustrated by a passage in the American journalist Thomas M. Johnson's *Secret War: Espionage and Counter-espionage*, published in 1930. Johnson offered the usual disclaimer for the book that he described as 'a substantially truthful account of Intelligence and Secret Service work abroad'. It was only 'substantially truthful', Johnson claimed, because he had 'forgotten purposely' a few details that might have been responsible for 'harming seriously some person or Government'. However, he divulged a technique by which the US Army communicated on field telephones towards the end of the war; that is, by using Native Americans who spoke languages unknown to the Germans. This passage may have seemed innocuous enough to relate in 1930, a dozen years after the guns fell silent on the Western Front. However, it is fortunate for the course of World War II – in which the US Marine Corps made prolific and successful use of Navajo code talkers in the Pacific Theater – that Johnson appears not to have had any Japanese readers.

Johnson claimed to have 'taken liberties' in his book with details such as names, places and dates (*TJ*, 7). Many other former spies also took liberties, and these memoirs can sometimes be frustratingly vague about the precise context of the exploits described. Everitt's work is full of sentences such as: 'The midnight express to — was crowded' and 'On arrival at — my taxi-cab was followed.' Such strategies make verification of their claims all but impossible, and one critic has denounced Victor Kaledin's memoirs as 'racy trash' that owe more to Saxe Romer's Fu Manchu novels than to historical reality.[5] In fact, the safest way for ex-spies to publish their work, a number of them quickly realized, was in novels. In *Ashenden, or The British Agent*, published in 1928, Somerset Maugham, who went to Russia in 1918 to serve as chief of British and American intelligence, disguised his experiences under the cover of fiction. He was careful, however, not to contravene the Official Secrets Act by giving away too much information, even between the covers of a novel.

The accounts that follow detail the spying game – secrets about codes, disguises, infiltration and other indispensable tactics – from the selected eight memoirs. They have been selected, first and foremost, for the insights they cast on international espionage and on the war effort in general. They have also been chosen in order to offer points of view from both the Allied and Central Powers. The authors include two British intelligence agents working separately in France; a half-British, half-Dutch agent running a train-watching operation on the Dutch–Belgian frontier; a British agent operating in Germany; a German agent undercover on the Eastern front; a Russo-German double agent in Russia and Germany; an Austro-Hungarian agent operating in Russia; and an American war correspondent attached to the American Expeditionary Forces in France.

However self-censorship may sometimes have stayed the pens of these spies, or fantasy and exaggeration spurred them on, their works make for undeniably fascinating reading. We learn about their distinctive and colourful disguises, such as the costumes of street hawkers, Jewish pedlars, and even a caviar salesmen whose silver-plated cigarette case was polished to such a high sheen that it could be used as a mirror through which to covertly observe the enemy. With so much of World War I fought in the agricultural lands of the Low Countries and Northern France, we encounter agents improvising in these rural areas by communicating through laundry spread out to dry, the rotation of a windmill's vanes, and even the furrows made by ploughs in farmers' fields. We see how even the most seemingly innocuous establishment, such as a patisserie, could become a nest of spies, with the baker-cum-spymaster signalling his agents by means of the special arrangement of pastries in his shop window. We are left, above all, with an impression of improvisation and ingenuity born of desperation and chaos in one of the dark periods of world history.

Melanie King, Oxford, 2013

Biographies

Lieutenant Alexander Bauermeister (Agricola), trans. Hector C. Bywater, *Spies Break Through: Memoirs of a German Secret Service Officer* (London: Constable, 1934).

Alexander Gustavovich Bauermeister was born in St Petersburg, Russia, in 1889, the son of a German businessman. When the First World War started, Bauermeister was twenty-five and an agent of the Abteilung IIIb, the secret service of the German military. After working undercover in St Petersburg, Oberleutnant Bauermeister, codenamed Agricola, was sent to Königsberg (now Kaliningrad). He became the most effective Germany spy on the Eastern Front, with his acquisition and decoding of Russian military communications greatly contributing to the German victory at Tannenburg in August 1914. He had many adventures on the Eastern front and was sent to Russia after the 1917 revolution to convince Russians not to continue fighting against the French and British. In the 1920s and 1930s he became a leading German authority on Soviet affairs, publishing articles in the German military journal *Deutsche Wehr*.

Bauermeister's book was first published in 1933 in Berlin as *Spione durchbrechen die Front* (Spies Break through the Front). It was translated into English the following year. Little is known about his subsequent activities. He died in Rome in 1940.

NICHOLAS EVERITT, *British Secret Service during the Great War* (London: Hutchinson, 1920).

Nicholas Everitt was born Henry Reeve Everitt in Norfolk in 1867. Before the war, he was a solicitor in Norwich and Lowestoft, residing first at North Cove Hall and then at Oulton Broad. When the Great War started, Everitt was forty-seven. He had been refused active service in Ireland the previous year due to his age, but was determined, despite this setback, to do his bit. He therefore wrote to the celebrated game hunter Frederick Courtney Selous with the idea of setting up a corps of 500 Big Game Hunters to be used as sharpshooters. Selous agreed to head the corps. However, the proposal was turned down out of hand by the War Office.

A keen wild fowl and geese hunter, Everitt had spent most summers before the war shooting in Scandinavia, in particular around the Danish–German borders. He knew the Danish and Schleswig-Holstein coasts and the islands of Heligoland from Holland to Denmark intimately. By the summer of 1914, when the Germans had mined this area, Everitt's knowledge of the region became invaluable; encouraged by his friend, Selous, Everitt reapplied to the War Office, offering his unique services. He was hired by the Secret Service, given the code name Jim, and sent to Scandinavia.

Everitt's memoirs are full of cynical overtones. This was partly because of what he saw as gross incompetence by the British authorities, and partly because he felt a lack of appreciation or recognition for the work he had undertaken. This applied especially to his invention which involved the design of camouflaged fishing trawlers that hid guns capable of sinking U-boats.

Nicholas Everitt died in 1928 at the age of sixty-one, and is buried in Norfolk. His marriage was annulled and there were no children. A waterfront park in Lowestoft bears his name.

THOMAS M. JOHNSON, *Secret War: Espionage and Counter-espionage* (London: Jarrolds, 1930).

Born in 1889, Thomas Marvin Johnson graduated from Hobart College in Geneva, upstate New York, in 1913. He first worked as a journalist on a local paper, the *Geneva Times*, before joining the *New York Sun*, a now-defunct newspaper best known for its perennially reprinted 1897 editorial 'Is There a Santa Claus?' Johnson was accredited to the American Expeditionary Force in October 1917, arriving at Neufchâteau to report on General Philippe Pétain's visit to the American headquarters. In 1918 he covered the American campaign against the Germans, at one point climbing a tree to watch the departure of American troops. The following year he attended the Paris Peace Conference.

After World War I, Johnson became a prolific freelance writer, authoring numerous books on espionage, including *Our Secret War: True American Spy Stories, 1917–1918* (1929), *Secret War: Espionage and Counter-espionage* (1930) and *Secrets of the Master Spies* (1932). He also published widely on the same topic in publications such as *Collier's Weekly*, *The Saturday Evening Post*, *The Reader's Digest*, and even *Modern Mechanix*. He lived long enough to write about Nazi and Russian spies in World War II, serving as a National Endowment for the Arts military writer during the war and in 1943 publishing *What You Should Know About Spies and Saboteurs*. He died in 1970, after which his friends funded a scholarship in his name at Hobart College.

COLONEL VICTOR KONSTANTINE KALEDIN, *K.14.–O.M.66: Adventures of a Double Spy* (London: Hurst & Blackett, 1934).

Victor Konstantine Cecil Luke de Mordowtzell Kaledin had a background and upbringing as exotic as his name. He was born in 1887 in the village of Glafirovka (now in the Ukraine). His mother was English, while his father Alexei was a famous Cossack general who at the outset of World War I commanded the 12th Cavalry Division. Following his mother's death, Kaledin was raised by a foster-mother of mixed Ukrainian and Gipsy descent, who took him at the age of eight to live with her tribe, the chieftain of which was a notorious drug and liquor smuggler who also worked undercover for the Ochrana, the Russian secret police. Kaledin boasted that he spoke Eÿgipta (Gipsy) jargon before learning Russian and that he had been taught wrestling, swimming and riding by the tribe.

At the age of fifteen, Kaledin was sent by his father to the Imperial Lyceum in Moscow. His first job was as a page to Tsar Nicholas II, but in 1909, at the age of twenty-two, he was transferred to the Secret Service in the Palace. After studying counter-espionage methods, Oriental languages (he was alleged to have mastered fifteen languages in all), together with other skills required for the Secret Service, Kaledin was sent to Russian Intelligence at St Petersburg. From there he was transferred to a Baltic intelligence bureau where he was to work on stemming pro-German support.

In 1914, Kaledin became a double agent and entered Germany under the alias Colonel Nicholas Mousin, posing as a commercial traveller and letting it be known that he was a disillusioned and drink-addled Russian officer. Successfully convincing the German authorities that he was pro-German, he was signed up as one of their spies. His career began in earnest when he gave the Germans the names of several Russian spies working in Germany.

By the early 1930s Kaledin and his English wife, Evelyn, were residing in the village of West Down in Devon. Kaledin published four other books besides *K.14.–O.M.66*. The first, *F-l-a-s-h D13*, purporting to be the inside story of the Tsar's secret service, was published in the UK by Cassell in 1931. The others included *High Treason: Four Major Cases of the St Petersburg Personal Court Branch* (1936), *Underground Diplomacy: Adventures of a Private Spy* (1938) and *The Moscow–Berlin Secret Files* (1940). He vigorously denied accusations of fictionalizing his work. By 1956, he was living in Norway. Fittingly for such a mysterious character, the date and whereabouts of his death are unknown.

CAPTAIN HENRY LANDAU, *All's Fair: The Story of the British Secret Service behind German Lines* (New York: G.P. Putnam's Sons, 1934).

Henry Landau was born in 1892 in the Orange Free State, Transvaal (Boer Republics), South Africa, to an English father and a Dutch mother. His entrepreneurial father owned a farm in the Transvaal, but after the end of the Boer War the family migrated to England. Landau was educated at Dulwich College, a German school in Dresden, Gonville and Caius College, Cambridge, and at the Colorado School of Mines. On the outbreak of the Great War, Landau saw service with the British Army on the Western Front. He entered the Secret Intelligence Service by chance, after dating the sister of his adjutant, who was employed in the army's Military Intelligence Department. Impressed that he spoke numerous languages, she suggested that he apply to the War Office. Passing the written and oral exams in Dutch, Landau joined the Intelligence Corps and was sent to the Belgian–Dutch border to reorganize a train-watching operation that had been shut down by the Germans. After the war, Landau worked on the Inter-Allied Intelligence Commission in Brussels, awarding medals and compensation to captured or executed agents. He moved on to the new passport control department in Berlin, but resigned in 1920. Thereafter he tried various business ventures, including writing. He died in Florida in 1968.

NICHOLAS SNOWDEN, *Memoirs of a Spy* (London: Jarrolds, 1934).

Nicholas Snowden was born in 1895 in a Hungarian city in the Carpathians, part of what in 1918 would become Czechoslovakia. His birth name was Miklós Soltész and he was one of four brothers and two sisters. His mother died when he was nine years old. Soltész possessed a natural flair for languages. He was fluent in Hungarian, Polish, Russian, Serbian, Bohemian, Ruthernian (the language of an Eastern Slavic ethnic group that lived in modern-day Russia, Belarus, Poland, Slovakia and Ukraine), Slovak, Croatian, German and French. Besides that, he spoke passable Romanian and Yiddish, and during the war he added English, Spanish and Italian to his repertoire.

In 1914, Soltész's uncle, a policeman, proposed his eighteen-year-old nephew for the Austro-Hungarian Secret Service. Soltész was accepted, no doubt because of his linguistic abilities, and his work was to concentrate on countries to the east and south of Russia, Romania and Serbia, which he entered undercover with the code name T43.

When the war ended, Soltész's homeland became the Republic of Czechoslovakia and he continued working as a spy, this time for the Czechs. Hungary was now headed by communist Béla Kun and all Czechs were mobilized against the Bolshevik threat. Soltész was sent undercover to Hungary to join the Bolsheviks. When Kun's government fell, Soltész was sent undercover to join the Hungarian–Slovak Legion in Hungary, which had its eyes on taking over Czechoslovakia. After capture and eight months in prison, followed by a short stint of business studies at the University of Prague, Soltész emigrated in 1923 to Argentina, and later to New York, where he spent the rest of his days boasting of his spying adventures as he worked as a barber in Manhattan. In 1933 C. Scribner's Sons published *Memoirs of a Spy*, with the author's name anglicized to Nicholas Snowden. The following year it was published in Britain.

CAPTAIN FERDINAND TUOHY, *The Secret Corps: A Tale of 'Intelligence' on All Fronts* (London: John Murray, 1920).

Ferdinand Tuohy was born in County Cork, Ireland, in 1891, and educated in France and Germany. In his early twenties he worked on the staff of the *Weekly Dispatch* in London. At the onset of war, however, he joined the British Intelligence Corps attached to the army, visiting theatres of war in France, Italy, Greece, Egypt, Palestine and Mesopotamia on special missions for the Wireless Signalling Corps. After the war he lived mainly in France, travelling frequently as foreign correspondent for *The Sphere*. After

Tuohy's wife Ann died in a tragic accident in 1929, he continued working as a foreign correspondent, contributing to numerous newspapers. During the Second World War, he presented the BBC's Empire programme on international affairs. He died in France in January 1952.

EDWIN THOMAS WOODHALL, *Spies of the Great War: Adventures with the Allied Secret Service* (London: John Long, 1932).

Edwin Thomas Woodhall was born in London in 1886. After a short stint in the army, he joined the Metropolitan Police Force at the age of twenty. Despite the fact that he was half an inch under the regulation height, an exception was made due his excellent physical fitness. From 1906 onwards, he held posts in the Special Political Branch, Secret Intelligence Police, and Protective Surveillance departments. He also worked alongside many officers who had once been assigned to the Jack the Ripper investigation in the 1880s. Woodhall was thirty-eight when war broke out, and was initially sent to Boulogne to guard the Prince of Wales, who was attached to the General Staff in France. After becoming chief of the Secret Police working with the Allies, he once famously dressed as a priest and chased and arrested Percy Topliss, the 'Monocled Mutineer', following a tip-off that he'd been seen drinking in a local bar. After the war, Woodhall left the Secret Intelligence Police and set up his own detective agency. He wrote over forty books, mainly on famous old crimes. He died penniless in London in 1941.

Quotations from the above works are indicated in parentheses in the text. For abbreviations, please refer to the Notes and References.

There is something so mysterious and thrilling about the Secret Service that the subject must inevitably appeal to the public, and especially to the more imaginative section of it. Experience gives point to the old saying that a man's ability is shewn less in never getting into a scrape, for *humanum est errare*, than in knowing how to get out of one! There is perhaps no vocation in which it is easier to get into a tight corner and more difficult to get out again than in the Secret Service, where the sword of Damocles often hangs over one's head.

Viscount Northcliffe, February 1920

I

A life of adventure?

'IN THE SECRET SERVICE one must paddle one's own canoe, alone and unassisted; always up-stream; always through dangerous rapids, wherein at every yard are hidden rocks and snags ready to tear the frail craft asunder; always through countries overrun with enemies armed with poisonous arrows which are fired singly and in volleys whenever the smallest opportunity is given; always hunted and stalked both day and night by the most persevering, cunning, and desperate huntsmen in the world; always on the move, with never a sure, safe, or secure resting-place for one's weary limbs; and always on the *qui vive* against a thousand and one unseen, unknown, and unsuspected dangers' (*NE* 173–4).

So wrote Nicholas Everitt, the Norfolk solicitor-turned-spy, in *British Secret Service during the Great*

War, published two years after the end of World War I. Everitt, an enthusiastic adventure-seeker, made espionage sound exciting. However, not all spies would have agreed with his claims about the constant danger, excitement and derring-do. Another British agent, Captain Ferdinand Tuohy, believed that 'an awful lot of bunkum' was written about secret service work. 'Spying is an unspectacular business', he claimed; 'it is often unutterably dull and sordid.' Many spies sold information as if it were a mere commodity; indeed Tuohy treated such a person as though he were selling a piece of cheese. The work was certainly less involved and mysterious than most people imagined (*FT*, 14, 40). Edwin Woodhall concurred: 'It was not all romantic ... Secret service work, like detective work, had its dull patches of routine, but that routine is necessary – vitally necessary – if success is to be assured' (*EW*, p. 37).

Woodhall, as an ex-policemen, appreciated the graft and tedium that spying often required. His own book, *Spies of the Great War*, gives an example of how a 'tedious vigil' outside the village of Fleurbaix in France paid dividends after three long nights. He was instructed to hide in order to keep watch for a spy known to be operating

nearby – but his experience was less cloak-and-dagger and more shawl-and-basket. Before dusk on two consecutive nights he noticed a little old lady hobbling by, clutching a small basket. On the third night Woodhall became suspicious and decided to shadow her. She led him to a ruined church: 'I followed her unobserved. She drew her shawl closely over her head, and entered the shell-blasted church door shortly after seven o'clock.

She went straight to a door in the tower and began gingerly to mount the dilapidated stairs, muttering and mumbling to herself in Flemish. I followed as cautiously as possible, striving to make no sound on the creaking boards. She must have been slightly deaf, for she had no idea that I was close behind her.'

Woodhall was astonished to find what appeared to be a British officer hiding in the ruins. However, even though the man's papers appeared genuine, his accent gave him away when he pronounced the word 'want' as *vont*. He was in fact a German spy, who, before the war, had worked in England as manager of a London hotel. The old woman had thought she was helping a genuine British officer and as such had concealed him for ten days (*EW*, 39–40).

Even more tedious was the assignment given to those who, as part of Henry Landau's espionage network, were charged with noting the arrivals and departures of railway units. When the Germans began moving troops by rail it could be an indication that an offensive was planned – and so keeping a close eye on the railways was essential. This trainspotting was often done from houses bordering the railways, frequently undertaken by

a husband-and-wife team. They would operate in
shifts, being careful to remain hidden from sight
during the day, and working in darkness at night.
These watchers had to be meticulous, noting
the composition of every train passing through,
including those carrying foodstuffs or other war
material. It was boring and monotonous work
but – as Landau observed – absolutely essential to
the war effort (*HL*, 65–6).

2

Tricks of the trade

'COMMUNICATION is one of the most important aspects of the secret service', wrote the war correspondent Thomas M. Johnson. 'A spy who cannot communicate his news in time is about as useful as no spy at all' (*TJ*, 133). But communication was far from easy. Agents in the field needed to pass messages back and forth to one another, but for security reasons they could not know one another's identities. Means had to be found by which these agents could be brought into contact with one another while still maintaining their anonymity.

Henry Landau operated what he called an 'octopus system'. The body of the octopus was known as a 'letter-box', a resident agent who co-ordinated the efforts of the agents in the field and received their intelligence. The tentacles were his local agents, who knew the letter-box but not each other. Various ingenious methods existed so that the agents could contact the letter-box and trade information anonymously without raising suspicions. It was the responsibility of the letter-box to signal when the coast was clear. Care had to be taken not to attract unnecessary attention from neighbours or the police. Landau instilled in his agents the necessity for a simple routine. If there was no danger in approaching the establishment, then the letter-box would leave a blind in a certain position or a flowerpot in the window. If it was unsafe to approach, the letter-box would change the position of the blind or remove the flowerpot. Occasionally, reports were thrown through an open window when passing, but only if this was sure not to attract unwanted attention (*HL*, 85–6).

Once reports had been delivered to the letter-box, an itinerant agent who travelled regularly to and from the country being spied upon would collect the reports. The resident agent or letter-box was typically a businessman, either neutral or a citizen of the enemy country. He would choose his agents personally – they could be a foreign music-hall artist, a voluntary Red Cross helper, a governess in a general's family, a barber living near a military camp, a shipping agent, a hotel attendant, or a corrupted soldier; in fact, anyone who was willing to collect information (*FT*, 11–12).

Victor Kaledin described an ingenious method by which a letter-box in Moscow contacted his agents, Kaledin included. The letter-box was a Polish baker, Ianash Vonsovsky, whose 'grimy' shop had a door sign featuring enormous wooden angels holding baskets of gilded cakes. Vonsovsky devised an unusual way of signalling that he was a letter-box where German agents could leave outgoing reports. Stale loaves needed to be marked with the municipal rejection stamp, and so Vonsovsky stacked these day-old loaves in a pile in the left hand corner of the shop window, thereby indicating that 'accredited German agents in Moscow could use the place as a "letter-box" for outgoing reports'. Victor Kaledin knew Vonsovsky but not that he was a letter-box until he noticed a signal specifically for him. In the window display was some *krendl* – sweetened pastry twisted into numbers from 1 to 100. Kaledin's German cipher, '66', lay next to the number '44'. This juxtaposition meant nothing to the average passer-by, but to Kaledin it indicated something very specific, since the number 44 'denoted a man with an important position in the Eighth Section (Central Russia) of the Berlin High Command. And this, coupled with the juxtaposition of my own cipher figures, told me that agent "44," having inside knowledge of my presence in Moscow, was there waiting for me and would continue to wait until I came' (*VK*, 141–2).

Agents were often required to make contact with one another without the assistance of a letter-box to bring them together. Nicholas Everitt described a typical encounter by which another agent made contact with him in Norway. 'At the appointed place and hour, I strolled casually into the entrance hall of a certain hotel and stood apparently puzzling over the railway and steam boat time-tables which were hanging on the wall. Several people were in evidence, but no one seemed to be particularly interested in anyone else. I had been there quite a time, and was wondering how I could explain my presence in order to excuse and justify a prolonged lingering, when I observed a small-built, quiet, inoffensive-looking young man cross the hall and stop near the hotel register. Absent-mindedly he tapped his teeth with his pince-nez, and muttered to himself and half aloud, "I wonder if Mr. Jim has called for that letter."'

'Mr Jim' was, of course, the password Everitt had been instructed to listen for. The unknown agent was to pass him certain orders without which he would have been 'like a ship in a gale minus the rudder'.

'The little man never looked at me nor even my way', Everitt wrote. 'He had stepped near enough so that I could overhear his *sotto voce*, also within range of two or three others who were congregated in the hall. His utterance was low, but it was as clear as a bell, and he spoke in Norwegian. No one took any notice of him or his remark. This, however, appeared to trouble him not a bit. Adjusting his glasses he pulled a newspaper out of his coat pocket and proceeded to make himself comfortable on a settee in a remote corner, where he could observe all that passed and all who came or went; provided he wished so to interest himself should the contents of his paper fail to hold his attention.

'Having marked down the man, there was no need to hasten matters. Caution at one's initiation is generally advantageous. Ten minutes later I seated myself on the same settee as the stranger and also became absorbed in a newspaper. Assuring myself that no one was within earshot

except the little gentleman before referred to, I murmured soft and low, whilst I still appeared to be reading the paper: "I know Mr. Jim. Can I give him the letter for you?"

"'Who sent you to ask for it?' the stranger queried. I named a name which was a countersign. "For whom does Mr. Jim require it?" I gave the third and final word which proved beyond doubt my title to the precious document.

'During this short conversation both of us had been studying our news-sheets, and unless an observer had been stationed within a few feet of us, nothing transpired that could have given the smallest clue to the fact that any communication had passed. With no sign of recognition the little man got up to go. He left his paper on the seat, and in passing me he whispered: "You will find the letter in my *Evening News*. Good luck to you"' (*NE*, 76–7).

The toothpick trick, noted by American war correspondent Thomas M. Johnson, was another way for one spy to pass a message to another. One spy would board a train on the French frontier and make his way to the dining car. Before leaving the table he would sit leisurely picking his teeth with a toothpick. At the first Swiss station, his accomplice would enter the dining car and take the seat that had just been vacated. Spy number two would order a meal, before long accidentally spilling some wine on the tablecloth. Apparently embarrassed, he would cover the spillage with a napkin and continue with his meal. However, before departing, spy number one had written a message on the tablecloth, using his toothpick filled with invisible ink. This message was developed by the

spilt wine. Having read it, spy number two would cover the message with his napkin until the words evaporated into thin air (*TJ*, 136).

A simpler method on trains, also reported by Johnson, was for one spy to hide a secret message in the padded seat arms when travelling on trains, to be extracted by another spy when safely across the border. To distract attention from the real hiding place, a trunk with a false bottom and filled with harmless items would act as a decoy (*TJ*, 139–40).

3

Languages of victory: secret codes

'WHEN SECRET SERVICE AGENTS are working abroad they must perforce rely upon codes of sorts, for means of intercommunication between themselves, their friends and supporters. These codes are invented by them entirely at their discretion. If they are wise in their generation they never keep the same code too long in use, but change it, at frequent intervals, for another entirely different in every respect. Such codes cannot be too carefully prepared; whilst every user knows that if his deception is discovered the consequences to himself might be serious indeed' (*NE*, 83).

Secret codes, as Nicholas Everitt points out in this passage, were a vital tool of the trade for spies, and something that needed to be created with ingenuity and used with caution. Those codes and ciphers used by intelligence services during the First World War ranged from simple to highly sophisticated. According to Captain Tuohy, British agents were known by letters of the alphabet – a simple enough system that was, however, made more complex by the fact that these letters were interchangeable and were 'worked out in connection with certain phases of the lunar system' (*FT*, 13).

In another code, naval vessels were given proper names. As Everitt wrote: 'To each was attached a definite meaning, and the message would be worded so that anyone seeing it would think it related to an ordinary everyday event. Christian names might be coded to mean definite objects; to wit – Bertha, a battleship; Dora, a torpedo boat destroyer; Sarah, a submarine; Tiny, a torpedo boat; Mary, a merchantman; Connie, a collier; Trina, a trawler; Louisa, an airship; and so on' (*NE*, 87). Merchant vessels, meanwhile, were designated by surnames. However, in another code, surnames designated numerals. According to Everitt, Oldman meant one; Turner, two; Truman, three; Smith, four; and so forth. Thus, a telegram handed in at Lowestoft that read 'Sent your housemaid Sarah Jones to Felixstowe 4 o'clock this afternoon', on being decoded, would read: 'Five submarines passed Lowestoft at 4 o'clock this afternoon steaming south' (*NE*, 87–8).

Everitt explained how information could be imparted in letters that seemed to be discussing something else entirely: 'Any reference to an illness meant that damage had been done, or that a vessel had been adversely affected to some extent. Any reference to a marriage or engagement meant that a combat or battle had taken place. "In bed" conveyed the news that a ship or ships had been sunk. "Put to bed" meant sunk, annihilation, or defeat, according to the context; mention of "delirium or head sickness" conveyed suspicions, or suspicious circumstances; "doctor called in" that the enemy (or others, as the context might convey) had retired, or been put to flight, whilst any direct, or indirect, reference to "remaining here, or at some named place," that the object or objects in question were still there or likely to remain' (*NE*, 88).

The perils of this kind of system of substitution are highlighted by the mistake made by a meddling Dutch telegraph operator. Everitt described how a message was once handed in to a telegraph office in Holland. The message, to be cabled to the United States, read simply: 'Father dead'. However, the telegraph operator, on his own initiative, perhaps to spare the feelings of the relatives by employing more elevated language, edited the cable to read: 'Father deceased'. A reply came back immediately: 'Is father dead or only deceased?' (*NE*, 119–20).

The Russians, meanwhile, concealed their messages by embedding them in other specialized languages. Kaledin reported that one intelligence chief, General N.S. Batioushin, believed that messages should be hidden in a natural background. For example, coded intelligence messages for the Seventh Section of the General Staff from Siberia were first sent to three furriers in St Petersburg. According to Batioushin the code combinations mixed with ordinary fur-trade language would not attract the attention of telegraph operators (*VK*, 204).

Train traffic was closely watched during the war, and the composition of troops trains was denoted, Landau observed, by a system of abbreviations: '"W" stood for the ordinary cattle trucks or wagons; "v" for the regular passenger coaches, or voitures; "w. plats" for flat trucks; "w. hausettes" for the high open trucks; and "w. baches" for wagons covered in tarpaulins. Thus a train conveying infantry might read: 10:15, 1 v. officers, 33 w. soldiers, 3 w. horses, 6 w. plats cars. An artillery unit might show the following composition: 1 v. officers, 10 w. soldiers 20 w. horses, 4 w. plats cannons, and 8 w. ammunition wagons' (*HL* 1, 66).

More complicated codes existed. Circular codes are notoriously difficult to break. The Prussian master spy who served under Otto von Bismarck, Wilheim Stieber, invented the famous 'lip and tooth' code which, according to the double agent Victor Kaledin, was adapted by Major von Lauenstein of the German intelligence service and introduced into the circular code. The circular code, as Kaledin described it, was a system of '*double flats* (short pauses) in between *guide words*', which the major claimed 'would baffle any foreign agent'. It very nearly baffled Kaledin despite his talents as a linguist.

Once when he was hospitalized during the war, he found himself in a bed next to a dying man whose 'vast head' and 'dark piercing eyes' looked 'tantalisingly familiar'. He soon recognized the man as a famous German spy, Abraam Rachoulka Portnoy, who went by the alias Karl Müller. Arrested by the Russians while working

in a munitions factory, Portnoy was now ill and
close to death. His last task was to tell Kaledin,
using code, where in the hospital his secret report
was hidden. Portnoy spoke in Yiddish, repeating
certain words. Kaledin understood this language
and listened carefully, but for a while remained
baffled as to its meaning. 'For a space I puzzled
ineffectually, seeking for some initial clue. Then

it struck me that all the vowels in the words used were five in number and the consonants twenty – the latter, discounting the purely diaphragmantic rumblings, divided roughly into eleven mutes and fourteen spirants'. Once Kaledin worked this out he quickly discovered the location of the report hidden in the bathroom of the hospital (*VK*, 38).

Ciphers needed to be changed regularly in case they were broken by the enemy. Thomas M. Johnson reported that American radio codes were only valid for three to six weeks, after which it could be assumed they had been cracked by the Germans. The Americans periodically tested their codes by sending fake messages such as ordering an 'attack' in a sector from which they had already withdrawn. If the Germans immediately attacked that sector, the code was changed immediately (*TJ*, 60–61).

The Americans had a secret weapon when it came to creating unbreakable codes. 'One brilliant expedient to confuse the Germans', wrote Johnson, 'was the sending to France of a specially picked detachment of American-Indians who, in dialects unknown in Germany, were to do all the confidential talking on American trench telephones.' The Navajo 'code talkers' used by

the US Marines against the Japanese are justly famous. But Native Americans were also used in World War I. The American Expeditionary Force included fourteen Choctaw-speaking soldiers who transmitted orders over the field telephones. Their usefulness was only realized in October 1918 by a US Army captain who overheard several of his enlisted men, soldiers from rural Oklahoma, speaking Choctaw. Since the Germans had broken the army's codes, the officer suggested that the Choctaws should be used to transmit messages on the field telephones. The US Army also began using members of other tribes for the same purpose, including the Cheyenne, Cherokee and Comanche, with similarly successful results: not one of their messages was ever decoded by the Germans (*TJ*, 63).[6]

4

*'Conceal me what I am':
identity and disguise*

ACCORDING TO the British spy Nicholas Everitt, 'So many people imagine that anyone and everyone who is engaged in detective or Secret Service work carries about with him a large assortment of wigs, false hair, and other disguises. When any of this work is reproduced on the stage or in moving pictures, or in the pages of works of fiction, disguises of various kinds are generally well to the fore. But gentle reader, take it from me, who have been through the real thing, and rest assured that any kind of disguise is always attended with danger. To wear false hair or wigs, or even to have them found in your possession, would mean death instantaneously, or at best next dawn, in an enemy country; probable imprisonment in a fortress for many years in a neutral one' (*NE*, 128).

That much said, Everitt did recognize the necessity of concealing one's identity through feigning,
for example, a different age: 'In real life it will be
found far easier to play the part of a person much
younger than it is to play the part of one who is
much older. For example, I would enter a building
to all outward appearances a man of sixty years of
age or upwards, and within a very short space of
time reappear as a man of not more than thirty.
These tricks may be attempted at night in artificial
lights, but by daylight the risks of discovery are
not worth the small gain or advantage that may
be believed to be attained by their aid' (*NE*, 128–9).

Another means of disguise, according to Everitt,
was adopting the persona of someone, such as a
sailor or workman, who would be unlikely to
attract attention: 'The common sailor, or working-
man who is badly dressed, very dirty in appearance and who has not shaved for many days, is
generally an object which most men avoid and
few women find the smallest interest in; whilst
he can roam at pleasure in most public places,
and if he has the price of a drink in his pocket
he invariably gathers around him a multitude of
friends ready to tell him anything they may know
or to believe any cock-and-bull story as to his

own antecedents which force of circumstances or a very vivid imagination may suggest' (*NE*, 129).

Everitt pointed out, however, that a member of the upper classes first needed to take some precautions before he disguised himself as a horny-handed son of toil. 'Before undertaking to appear as a unit of the working-classes', he wrote, 'it is advisable to take on a job which will put one's hands into the condition that would appear compatible to one's outward appearance.' He believed that rough physical labour, such as unloading or loading bricks, was the best means of achieving a convincing set of callouses. 'In a few hours, hands which are unaccustomed to this work will crack up and blister beyond recognition. Its continuance for a couple of days will pull the nails out of shape and give the full, true, horny, hardened grip of a genuine son of toil' (*NE*, 130).

Other spies were much more willing than Everitt to experiment with disguises and false identities. On his first espionage trip into Russia, the Austro-Hungarian spy Miklós Soltész was instructed by his intelligence chief, Captain Baron Ferdinand von Kirchens, to dress in the clothes of a Jewish pedlar. For his next assignment, a different disguise was adopted: 'On my second service trip I was dressed in Austrian uniform but I carried a Russian uniform with me into which I was to change before crossing the enemy's lines.' Both disguises kept him safe (*NS*, 29–33).

The double agent Victor Kaledin opted for a variety of different disguises. On one occasion in the Siberian city of Irkutsk he realized that he needed to infiltrate a gold smeltery from which messages in Morse code were being transmitted. The smeltery stood on Kharlámpievskaÿa Street, 'in an unsavoury strip of filled-in ground, amid a huddle of log cabins, ash dumps, piles of coal, pools of oil and water, electric cranes, and the bleaching ribs of abandoned barges' (*VK*, 215.) Kaledin soon learned that the key to getting information about the smeltery was the assistant foreman, Ossip Gavrik, who was a drug addict. He therefore stood outside the factory gates disguised as a street vendor, carrying a basket of what appeared to be liver pies, which he peddled at five gold roubles apiece. The nut-brown crust looked appetising and no different from any other hawker's pie, but Kaledin's pies included some special ingredients: some contained a paper ball of morphine, a few had hard-boiled egg mixed with cocaine, while others contained opium, sulphonol and veronal.

Kaledin was able to exploit Gavrik's and other of the workers' addictions, receiving information about the smeltery in return for the illegal drugs (*VK*, 216).

Not only did Kaledin sell liver pies to the smeltery workers as their shifts changed, but he also supplied cigarettes and shag, a coarse-cut tobacco, to other potential informants. For this activity, he acquired a 'picturesque costume' from members of the Siberian underworld, 'that strange fraternity of gaol-birds' who had no truck with the legal authorities. Kaledin's attire consisted of a new leather *zipoun* (native coat), 'Moscow boots', a blue cloth cap, and a shiny brass licensed hawker's badge. The Siberian mafia tolerated Kaledin and his spying so long as he did not intrude on their activities by preaching to prostitutes, berating pimps or – worst of all – turning members of the 'fraternity' in to the authorities (*VK*, 215–16).

Kaledin's street-hawker disguises were part of a long tradition of Russian espionage. His book *Adventures of a Double Spy* describes how the Russian Secret Service had used a technique known as 'packing' since at least 1887. In order to prevent a mission from miscarrying, the Secret Service would fill the streets in the relevant

neighbourhood with undercover agents disguised as street sweepers, pedestrians and cart-drivers, all of whom, as they pretended to go about their business, could watch the operation unfold and, if necessary, intervene (*VK*, 100–101).

Kaledin also possessed other disguises at his disposal. In the Russian port city of Taganrog he disguised himself as a wealthy caviar merchant.

And since beggars were a common sight in Irkusk, when on assignment in the Siberian city he decided to assume the attire of one of them for a planned burglary of a Russian general's residence. He described his adopted guise: 'I wore a ragged cotton *lopacha* (cloak), with a moth-eaten pony-hide collar; fur boots with double jute-soles; and a fur cap with a leather mask half-covering the face.' This half-mask had several advantages. Often it was to conceal some incurable illness, which meant people would give the wearer a wide berth. Moreover, the false matted beard worn by Kaledin hid small rubber containers filled with red thermit (a compound of iron oxide and powdered aluminium). When combined with magnesium powder and lit with a match, this small bomb was capable of producing a massive explosion at 5,400 degrees Fahrenheit. As the heat concentrated on the spot without spreading, it was suitable for attacking the steel plates of a safe. As an extra precaution, Kaledin also carried other house-breaking tools, including an 18-inch jemmy.

Kaledin's disguise served him well, albeit with some improvisation. Safely negotiating the garden wall of the general's residence, he thought everything was going according to plan. The gruff voices and unmistakable sound of heavy boots marching on hard-trodden snow proved otherwise. There was no time to escape so Kaledin was forced to think quickly. Loosening the belt of his cloak, he scooped a hole in the snow and squatted down to relieve himself. Within seconds he was surrounded by the police who threatened him with three months' hard labour for breaking the sanitary regulations. Kaledin pretended to be ill in the stomach with worms, and for added effect scratched himself in an exaggerated frenzy. The policemen thought this amusing and ordered him to the nearest police station to be cleaned and disinfected (*VK*, 205–12).

Kaledin was evidently adept at feigning illness – which became yet another of his disguises. When the Germans wanted Kaledin to help prisoners of war escape from the hospital in Tzarskoe-Selo, situated some fifteen miles from St Petersburg in Russia, he decided to get admitted as a patient himself. Entering a pharmacy he asked for a popular shampoo made from olive oil and Castile soap. As the pharmacist wrapped the bottle, Kaledin faked stomach cramps and groaned as if in pain. He asked the pharmacist for medicine for gastric cramps, but as the man went to his workroom

to make up the prescription, Kaledin used the shop telephone to call the Consulate, requesting a car to pick him up immediately. Kaledin then drank the contents of the shampoo bottle. When the Consulate car arrived, the double agent was writhing in genuine pain; he was carried to the car and taken immediately to the hospital (*VK*, 32).

Another disguise that Kaledin assumed was the identity of a deceased fellow agent. While in the hospital bed cleverly earned by ingesting that bottle of shampoo, Kaledin was passed a message by the person in the bed beside him, Abraam

Portnoy, who died soon afterwards. Kaledin knew that Portnoy was not a Polish Jew – as his papers claimed – but in fact the German agent Karl Müller. At this point Kaledin executed, as he boasted, 'a daring stroke of counter-espionage against the enemy I pretended to serve': he took on Portnoy's identity. He instructed an orderly, an obliging peasant, to daub red ink on the inside and outside of Portnoy's ears, which would signal to the Russian intelligence agent attached to the morgue that another agent was assuming the identity of the deceased (*VK*, 39).

Miklós Soltész also perpetrated this kind of identity theft on another of his undercover forays, this time to deliver a coded message to Hermann Kusmanek, a German general. Arriving in Przemyśl (in present-day Poland) he found himself caught in the last moment of battle between the Russians and the Germans: 'Guns crackled, fire flashed, hand grenades roared' (*NS*, 91). When daylight broke, Soltész, who had been hit by shrapnel, saw the wounded and the dead on the battlefield. 'Two soldiers lay not far away, one an Austrian, the other a Russian. The pain I was enduring made me unable to stand on my badly swollen leg, but I dragged myself toward the Russian soldier so that

I might discover the number of his regiment by the insignia on his tunic.'

The ill fortune of the dead Russian, Alexander Ivanovich Smolensky, turned out to be Soltész's good luck. 'Instantly I resolved to take his identification discs and all his other papers and belongings, so he would become an unknown soldier and I an impostor in his person. I searched him and took from him every identification paper which he possessed. Also, I took his tunic and put it on my own shoulders. He wore eyeglasses and these I took. I found they fitted me well enough to serve wonderfully well as camouflage. The little money he had in his pocket I left there. I did not need that, for I had plenty of my own, and what I had done was done only as a measure of safety to protect myself and the mission which had been committed to me.' From then on, Soltész was to be Alexander Ivanovich Smolensky (*NS*, 91–92).

The use of stolen, faked or otherwise false papers to complete a disguise was, of course, widespread. The American war correspondent Thomas M. Johnson claimed to have come across all sorts of reports regarding the use of false papers. 'False passports were often real ones, altered', he wrote. 'Many were taken from Allied civilians interned in Germany. Submarines took them from crews of neutral ships.' The Germans bought passports in Switzerland, and Johnson claimed a group of Russian Jews in Christiania, present-day Oslo, sold passports for ten dollars. The Germans also manufactured fake passports in a cellar in Geneva. But faked passports could be acquired, it seemed, virtually anywhere. 'Off in the Far East,' Johnson wrote, 'at Tientsin, under a floor in a Taku street fish-stall the Germans kept a store of Italian and Dutch passports obtained at the Peking lega-tions by men hired to ask for them for pretended journeys' (*TJ*, 139).

5

Eat, drink and be merry, for tomorrow we spy

A SPY needed to be extremely wary about accepting food or drink from strangers – and he (or she) also needed to be adept at getting strangers to eat or drink. As the smelters discovered when they purchased Victor Kaledin's pies, food and drink were often carefully and deliberately contaminated. And, as Kaledin knew, no one made an easier and more desperate informant than a drug addict.

Thomas M. Johnson recalled how the Germans came up with a 'devilishly simple' method of getting information from young American pilots. The German weapons, he wrote, 'were that worthy pair, cocaine and loose women'. Beautiful young women, 'all utterly abandoned', were hired to prey on the cadets, who, with cash in their pockets and their lives daily on the line, would be looking for ways to unwind. Pitying the '*pauvres garçons* their taut faces and twitching nerves', the women would lead them to private apartments where they produced liquors to drink and powders to help them relax. Drugged without their knowledge, the soldiers became addicts like the gold smelters. As such, they were vulnerable to the designs of anyone seeking information (*TJ*, 84).

Johnson reported a clever ruse used by one American agent to avoid getting drunk on the job: drinking a four-ounce bottle of olive oil beforehand. Providing it was consumed in time, it lined the stomach and protected the spy from the adverse effects of alcohol, keeping him sober and clear-headed. 'I was always sick next morning,' the agent reported, 'but I usually had my information' (*TJ*, 169)

Nicholas Everitt was also able to use alcohol to his advantage when he was spying in Denmark. He extracted important information from the unsuspecting enemy merely through pretending to be in a drunken post-prandial slumber.

'Danes, generally speaking, are heavy drinkers. They have a fondness for spirits, particularly with their coffee. It was advisable to wait until after the midday meal, when it was customary to repair to the smoke-room, if further curiosity was to be satisfied. Securing a corner seat I cocked up both my legs on to the settee and buried myself in a book – *Sagas of the North*. After ostentatiously appearing to drink a number of small glasses of spirits, signs of somnolescence followed. Soon the book dropped with a bang on the floor and intermittent snoring became almost a nuisance to the only two other occupants of the saloon, the Danish travellers.

'The confined space of the apartment caused them by compulsion to sit within a few feet of where I was lying. They had been whispering in so low a tone that not a word could be heard. As the snoring increased they raised their voices. Under the impression that the sleep was probably alcoholic, they were soon discussing their affairs in distinctly audible tones. And very interesting business it turned out to be.

'Shortly, it concerned the purchase, transport, and delivery of some hundreds of horses which they had been buying for and on behalf of, or for resale to, the German Government. This business had apparently been going on for some time. Denmark and Sweden had been early denuded

of all available horseflesh at enormous prices. Norway was now being swept clean' (*NE*, 78–9).

Miklós Soltész likewise used drink to his advantage – although in his case it was tea spiked with anaesthetic. On one mission, a female spy working alongside Soltész was captured, imprisoned and guarded by soldiers while awaiting execution. Time was of the essence and it was imperative

that she be freed. Soltész's cunning plan involved pouring a large quantity of a hypnotic liquid into a huge hot water boiler that was bubbling away, ready for the soldiers' tea.

'Standing there nonchalantly, I poured the drug mixture into the hot water boiler, and withdrew a few steps to watch breathlessly for developments. A few moments later the soldier came out again with a large container which he filled with hot water from the boiler. Then, indeed, the next twenty minutes of waiting seemed interminable. At last I passed around the house and looked in through a side window. By the dim light in the room I saw that all the soldiers were lying on the floor unconscious, seven of them in no condition to make trouble for us.'

Soltész concentrated on the two sentries guarding the spy in the anteroom. Using a piece of paper to direct its flow, he poured ether under the anteroom door. Within a short space of time the sentries also collapsed in a heap on the floor, overcome by fumes (NS, 109–10).

6

The walls have ears: eavesdrops and wiretaps

SPYING WAS OFTEN a high-tech operation in World War I, especially when it involved eavesdropping. Early on in the war, microphones were used by the British on the Western Front to listen to German conversations in the trenches. This developed into the new technique of flash and sound ranging, making it possible to plot the location of German artillery batteries. Sound ranging determined the coordinates of the batteries by using data derived from the sound of the guns, mortar or rockets. Microphones were used to produce a bearing to the source of the sound, and the intersection of these bearings gave the location of the battery. The bearings themselves were derived from the differences in the time of their arrival at the microphones. Locations obtained were then verified by aeroplane. 'What we couldn't hear,' wrote the journalist Thomas M. Johnson, 'we might see' (*TJ*, 63).

The Germans introduced a listening apparatus called the 'Moritz' which allowed them to intercept messages on British field telephones at the front by tapping into their telephone lines. The British Army responded by developing its own listening set, the 'Itok' or 'It'. Each consisted of a small box with wire leads that were positioned in no-man's-land. The box itself was deposited in a dugout near the front line where two interpreters wearing telephone headgear would sit listening day and night to the conversations in the enemy's trench. Any useful conversation overheard would be scribbled down and the daily listening sheets analysed by intelligence officers. The German operators became so adept at recognizing accents that, according to Captain Ferdinand Tuohy, they were able to determine whether the troops were English, Scottish, Welsh, Irish, Canadian or Australian (*FT*, 268–9). The Itok was ultimately used to mislead the Germans by the carrying out of fake conversations supposedly revealing secret information. However, when the Germans began doing the same and the British themselves were duped, the Itok became redundant (*FT*, 269).

Another technique of intercepting telephone calls, according to Victor Kaledin, was the Heinsel–Raub wire, an early but evidently effective version of wire-tapping. While on a mission in the port city of Taganrog, on the Sea of Azov, Kaledin witnessed preparations by the Greek community for a religious festival. One local restaurant owner, Gerasimos Koundouris, draped the oleograph portraits of the tsars with multicoloured flags. Suspecting Koundouris of some covert activity, Kaledin took out his silver cigarette case, which he used as a mirror to watch with his back turned as the Greek restaurateur went about his business. 'I saw Koundouris force a small red flag into the thick papier-mâché frame of the oleograph nearest to me. The flag itself was triangular in shape, and possessed a thin wire stem that swiftly attracted my attention, and then caused me an excited thrill. In a flash the truth came home to me: the flag's stem was a Heinsel–Raub wire, which when inserted into the wires of a telephone circuit, automatically prevented the instrument from ringing, and, with the current at a short or released stage, rang a similarly equipped telephone in some spy bureau; incidentally, without the knowledge of the exchange' (*VK*, 51).

A Belgian physics professor working for Henry Landau's intelligence operation came up with another means of electronic spying. He pointed out that messages could be intercepted from German telephones 'if earth was used as a return circuit in a field telephone', with the covert British connecting wire running parallel to the German one. He planned to implement one such set of intercepting wires in the Maastricht sector of the Belgian–Dutch border, where a river separating the two countries was at one point under very little surveillance. The professor's plan was to run wires underground between two cottages a hundred yards apart, one on the Belgian side and another on the Dutch side. The Dutch cottage owner was pro-Belgian and agreed to keep prying eyes away from the apparatus. However, the Armistice was signed before the operation could be completed (*HL* 1, 119–20).

The front line was not the only place where listening devices were used to eavesdrop on the enemy. Captain Tuohy reported how British agents, in order to listen to German prisoners of war, installed a listening device in and around the cage or outside the prison cell. Microphones were placed in the centre of the cage with buried

cables leading back to the listening operator's hut nearby. Inside the hut there would be several men with earphones who jotted down everything they heard while the prisoners chatted away, oblivious to the hidden ears (*FT*, 256–7).

In some cases, the German prisoners of war were only too happy to talk to the British. The ranks of the German Army included Poles and Danes and the inhabitants of Alsace-Lorraine, while the Prussians incorporated Saxons and other south Germans into their battalions. None of these conscripts was particularly fond of or loyal to their pay masters. Intelligence officers always made a point of interrogating Polish prisoners first, as they were often happy to talk, while the French took on the men from Alsace-Lorraine. Thomas M. Johnson recalled how the German commander, General Fuchs, ordered the relief of the 77th Reserve Division a few days before the battle of Saint-Mihiel (fought 12–15 September 1918) because so many of his troops had deserted to the Americans (*TJ*, 50).

The most valuable prisoner of all to the Allies was a German deserter. Many German troops deserted and, in doing so, eagerly revealed valuable secrets. According to Captain Tuohy, two or three a night crossed the wire into British lines, and scores were shot by the Germans while attempting to reach their goal. It was necessary, however, to be on guard against a 'deserter' being sent deliberately to deceive by imparting false information (*FT*, 267).

Interrogating prisoners in the heat of battle was never as successful or reliable as when examining a prisoner over a period of time. In the latter case, according to Captain Tuohy, the interrogator could plan his approach in detail. The ensuing battle of wits, interrogator versus prisoner, was challenging and exciting. Tuohy recalled sitting opposite a prisoner, taking out a sheaf of documents, similar to a solicitor trying to get the truth from a prospective divorcee, and beginning the interview (*FT*, 257). Certain rules were followed when interrogating prisoners. According to the *New York Sun* correspondent Thomas M. Johnson, the prisoner was always questioned on an empty stomach, in his own language, alone, and without being allowed to take notes (*TJ*, 52).

When the Allies were attempting to listen in on German prisoners who were unhelpfully sitting silent in their cage, a 'pigeon' would be introduced. This was either a renegade German or an Englishman who spoke perfect German and wore a German uniform. His duty was to direct the conversation in order to reveal true feelings and military strategies. The 'pigeon' might start talking about military losses, lack of food in his unit, or unfair discipline that he had seen or experienced. This often provoked the other prisoners to complain in turn. The operators listening with their earphones busily noted down everything as the prisoners complained among themselves (*FT*, 257).

According to Henry Landau, priests were used to listen to confidences and report back to intelligence chiefs. Sometimes they were sent into the cells to say prayers for the devout and, having listened to confidences, would relay messages to the authorities – something that clearly violated the sanctity of the confessional. At other times a priest would be introduced into a prison cell, masquerading as a fellow prisoner. Before he was flung into the cell, there would be theatrics outside – blows, shrieks of pain and angry taunts of 'dirty spy' – to convince the prisoners he was one of them and could be trusted (*HL* 1, 84).

Refugees were also used by both sides as spies or as sources of information. Intelligence officers would glean from them details about their native villages in the zone that was to be attacked, and where possible hiding places such as cellars were located, together with their size – vital information when planning an attack or in readiness for counter-attack. The Germans were discovered to be using refugee children as spies and infiltrating them into groups of French evacuees. 'Suspicion naturally would not rest readily on a child,' wrote Captain Tuohy, 'and yet seldom is one more observant than when still in one's teens' (*FT*, 105–6).

Other victims of the war – dead soldiers – also proved valuable sources of information. The battalion, regiment and division could be ascertained from the papers and insignia on a dead soldier. Tuohy explained what happened when the Allies recovered the bodies of dead German soldiers: 'On a dead man being brought in by our patrols, his identity disc would first be removed. This was the surest guide to the man's identity and regiment. Next, the shoulder strap bearing a number or monogram would be cut off the victim's tunic or greatcoat, and the marking on arms, clothing and equipment duly noted down. Finally, the dead man's pay-book, and all maps, letters, diaries, postcards, notebooks, etc., found upon him would be removed and the whole collection bundled up and forwarded to Divisional Headquarters.' Often clothing and effects would be soaked in blood and mud, making the examination process difficult and distressing. During busy times, HQ could receive up to fifty sacks of written material a day, and each would be scrutinized in detail in order to discover information about the enemy. Of particular value, according to Tuohy, were any personal letters on the deceased. 'The German was a great correspondent and usually carried on his person letters and postcards from dozens of comrades in other divisions and Corps.' It was the capture of one such postcard, he claimed, that gave Marshal Foch the first indication that the Germans were going to attack in May 1918, on the Chemin des Dames. But Tuohy noted the poignancy of going through the personal effects of a dead man: 'The dead man seemed to lose type and nationality. He ceased to be a Hun; he was just a dead man' (FT, 235–7).

Another source of information for the Allies was unexploded German ordnance. The recovery of these shells was one of the more dangerous acts of intelligence work – Tuohy called it the 'most disconcerting'. He claimed that there was at GHQ a 'quiet, bespectacled major' who wanted to know about every dud, 'wherever they chanced to have fallen, in trench or field, town or wood'. It was necessary to examine their fuses in order to gauge the munitions situation in Germany. Their contents would be chemically examined to ascertain whether new gas mixtures were being used. 'As the war became more and more an artillery contest,' wrote Tuohy, 'it behoved us to follow every German shell or fuse innovation most minutely, lest "Fritz" should steal a vital march upon us' (*FT*, 244–5).

Sometimes unexploded ordnance could be the result of industrial sabotage carried out by spies. Miklós Soltész explained how he was able to infiltrate ammunitions factories in Russia, 'secretly corrupting workmen and inducing them to make defective shells which would not explode'. When the Russians fired one of their duds, the German soldiers would remark: 'Our friends have mailed us another dead letter' (*NS*, 153).

7

The female of the species

WOMEN HAVE PROVED themselves effective as spies throughout history, from Aphra Behn, who spied for King Charles II, to 'Wild Rose' Greenhow, the well-connected Washington society hostess whose information has been credited with helping the Confederacy win both the First Battle of Bull Run and the Battle of Manassas in the American Civil War. The most famous spy of World War I was undoubtedly Mata Hari, the Dutch exotic dancer executed by the French in 1917 for being a German spy.

Not everyone, however, believed women made the best spies. According to Captain Ferdinand Tuohy, the French employed more women as spies in World War I than the British 'because women are more intelligent in France' (*FT*, 12). On the whole, however, Captain Tuohy was far from convinced that women – even 'intelligent' French women – should be used as spies. 'Most women spies are fundamentally unreliable', he wrote, 'and few of them can ever have been trusted with real secrets.' He believed that they lacked patience, method and concentration. He considered their technical and studious abilities poor, regarded them incapable of working out of the limelight, and declared them generally unsuitable for the demanding work required of a spy. Moreover, he believed a woman was likely to be indiscreet, following her heart rather than her head, with potentially disastrous results. Tuohy conceded that a woman might have a few advantages over a male colleague, in that she was far more deceitful, possessed greater intuition, and could use her looks to dupe a man (*FT*, 20–21).

The American war correspondent Thomas M. Johnson also thought that employing females was a 'gamble'. He acknowledged that they had 'more aptitude for deceit than men' – but this advantage was undermined by other typically female qualities. Allied Secret Service chiefs with whom he worked supposedly told him that women spies had three main drawbacks. First of all, they tended to exaggerate, especially in their military reports, which were often inaccurate and therefore useless. Second, as the female sex was more delicate than the male, women tended to fall victim to nervous strain and fatigue, and would also quickly become bored with the monotony of spy work. Finally, they would often fall in love with the very man on whom they have been assigned to spy – 'whereupon they become worse than valueless' (*TJ*, 251–2).

In Henry Landau's opinion, the beautiful female spy was far from essential and was in fact rarely involved in Secret Service work. For every Gabrielle Petit or Louise de Bettignies – famous female spies who lost their lives – there were a hundred male spies, not as glamorous perhaps, but equally brave and efficient (*HL* 1, 156).

The German spy codenamed Agricola at least believed female spies did one thing better than their male counterparts. 'A female spy who is being led to execution comports herself, as a rule, with greater courage than her masculine colleague', he wrote. 'Mata Hari (Margaret Zelle), Gabrielle Petit and Edith Cavell all faced rifles of the firing squad without a tremor, while, on the other hand, not a few male spies howled like beasts and had to be forcibly propelled to the place of execution' (*AB*, 16).

Johnson and Captain Tuohy may have doubted their abilities, but Miklós Soltész told the story of one female spy who very nearly proved effective and deadly. He encountered her, a beautiful young woman, as he crossed the Hungarian frontier by train. As the train arrived at Pragerhof railway station, the young woman entered his compartment, which contained reserved seating only. When asked to leave the carriage, she refused, claiming that she was desperate to reach the front line and volunteer as a Red Cross nurse. Partial to a pretty face, the senior officer travelling with Soltész agreed that she could sit with them as far as the Italian border.

In the early hours of the morning the young woman, who had drifted off in one of the seats adjacent to Soltész, suddenly began talking in her sleep and was heard to mutter: *Tutti gli Austriaci sono ladri*! (All Austrians are thieves!). Soltész understood her words and moved closer to listen further. As he did so, his attention was aroused by the brooch on her black dress. It was large and thick and made of black glass in the form of a woman's head. Carefully, Soltész removed the brooch from her dress while she slept and, loosening the glass, extracted the head. To his amazement, he spotted a piece of fine silky paper, tightly folded in the base. Suddenly awake, the woman made a dash for the door. The officer who had allowed her into the compartment grabbed her arm in an attempt to stop her, but with her free hand she stabbed him with a hat pin and, managing to escape his grasp, jumped out of the moving train.

What had she been hiding? Nothing less than a detailed plan of the Austro-Hungarian defensive works along the Adriatic coast, including the port of Fiume. For this to fall into the hands of the Italians would have been disastrous for the Austro-Hungarian forces (*NS*, 183–7).

Other female spies included a pair of nuns. The White Lady Intelligence train-watching network in Holland and Belgium was operated by 1,200 individuals. Henry Landau described how two of their agents were Sœur Marie-Melanie and Sœur Marie-Caroline. After their religious order had been expelled from France, they had been rehoused in a convent in Chimay, on the French border. 'There were no keener agents', observed Landau. 'Intelligent and resourceful, they knew how to make full use of their opportunities.' The convent had become a German military hospital;

while the two nuns were not expected to nurse the wounded, they were permitted to run a small shop where they could sell postcards and other items to the convalescing officers and soldiers, who engaged them in conversation. In the course of their work they were able to collect all sorts of useful information, which they passed on to the White Lady (*HL* 2, 92).

Another reputed female spy was a fortune-teller in Mayfair. Captain Ferdinand Tuohy writes about how he received a report that a fortune-teller, Madame Trost, 'a wicked old German woman' who ran a beauty parlour off Bond Street, was extracting information from the wives of British officers. Anxious about the fate of their husbands on the Western Front, the young women would consult Madame Trost, whose cryptic questions about the officers evidently raised the suspicions of several of her 'fair and innocent' young clients. However, Captain Tuohy – ever doubtful about female spies – was suspicious of these reports, dismissing most of them as scares that came to nothing (*FT*, 40).

Women were also used as what Victor Kaledin called 'illuminates'. These were spies used to ferret out information from officials, diplomats or generals that could be used against them. These spies were often women, paid to make friends with the female companions of their targets. Their brief was to discover if there was anything about the officials, such as the previous embezzlement of government funds, that could be 'used to blackmail the guilty party into giving away valuable data'. The guilty party would then have no choice but to pass on valuable data to the enemy (*VK*, 58).

8

Tools of the trade

ESPIONAGE AGENTS equipped themselves with a variety of implements to assist them in their covert activities. The Russian double agent Victor Kaledin regularly used a small detectascope, issued to him by the Russian Secret Service. This 'handy little contrivance' was equipped with a globular, fish-eye lens of less than a quarter of an inch in diameter, which could be inserted 'with the utmost care' into a crack in a door or window. By focusing the lens of this clever device, he was able to see shadowy outlines in the room (*VK*, 52).

Kaledin also had another invaluable piece of kit. Every Russian agent, he claimed, carried a service master-key – a thin wire hook. This tool came in useful on numerous occasions. On one assignment, looking for information that was to be passed to him, he noticed a little brass grid in the waste pipe at the bottom of the bath. The grid was wet and slippery, but he was able to unscrew it. He lowered the wire hook gently down the pipe until it caught on something. After he gave it a sharp tug, soap suds and brown disinfectant bubbled up, followed by a thin roll of oiled green silk, three-quarters of an inch in diameter and about five inches long – exactly the information he had been looking for (*VK*, 40).

Nicholas Everitt, on assignment in Belgium, where he was registered in a hotel as a 'fish merchant of Scandinavian origin', used an even more low-tech type of apparatus to see if he was being spied upon. 'The hair test', he claimed, 'is a useful expedite for gauging the inquisitiveness or prying proximities of one's immediate neighbours.' All one needed was a little wax and a couple of hairs. A single human hair, he wrote, 'is practically invisible to the naked eye, and a slight strain will snap it. If cunningly placed across the two covers of a box, on the lid of a box, over an unlocked bag, trunk suit-case or elsewhere, few Paul Prys would ever dream of suspecting its presence, and the precaution inevitably tells its own tale.' Everitt set up his hair trap and then retired outside to an 'arboreal retreat' to wait and see what he might catch (*NE*, 119–20).

Human hair could come in useful in other ways as well, in particular for female agents. Agent Agricola pointed out that many women concealed messages in their long tresses, as 'bobbing' had not yet come into fashion (*AB*, 21). Landau pointed out that men as well as women could hide messages about their person. Reports written on *papier pelure* – fine tissue paper – were hidden in hat bands, in the lining of clothing, and in shoes (*HL* 1, 62). The last came in useful for Miklós Soltész. In October 1914, as the Austro-Hungarian fortress of Przemyśl came under siege from the Russians, Soltész was given a coded document that he was instructed to deliver across the lines into Przemyśl. He was to wear a Russian uniform and the message was to be hidden in a waterproof rubber container placed inside a hollow in the heel of his Russian soldier's boot. The hollow in the heel was covered with leather and virtually undetectable (*NS*, 88).

At other times, Soltész would sew messages into compartments hidden between the lining of his belt and the fabric of his Russian trousers (*NS*, 52). He also secreted them in one of his military coat buttons when travelling back from Przemyśl to army headquarters. The button was ingeniously split into two halves that were hollowed out and fitted together by compression. The plan of operation would be written on silk tissue rolled into a tiny ball to fit inside the button (*NS*, 115).

Agricola, meanwhile, reported finding a message concealed in a suit of clothes worn by a suspected spy arrested near the front. The man had already been searched, to no avail, when Agricola arrived on the scene and noticed that he was wearing 'a brand-new suit of good quality, on which a patch had been sewn'. The patch raised his suspicions, which were unallayed when the suspect explained that he had torn his suit. Out came Agricola's knife. 'As I cut the stitches a scrap of paper fell to the ground. The paper was a fragment of a Russian Staff map upon which our various artillery positions were clearly marked with a cross' (*AB*, 93).

Agricola also discovered that walking sticks were often used as secret receptacles for messages. The top would be sawn off, hollowed out, and glued on again so skilfully as to defy all but the closest scrutiny. 'Only during the first month were we deceived by such crude and primitive devices' (*AB*, 21). Another primitive method that Agricola discovered was the use of watches: 'Early in the war Russian agents sometimes hid their messages in watches, usually behind the inner casing.' There was, however, a serious drawback – the watch stopped working as soon as the message was inserted. (*AB*, 93–4).

Yet another of the 'crude methods' used by the Russians and discovered by Agricola involved the use of wigs. 'In the Russian frontier town of Mlava', he wrote, 'there existed a peculiar Jewish sect. As the men had no special confidence in the fidelity of their wives, it was customary on the eve of a wedding to shave the head of the bride, and from that time until her death she had to wear a wig. This was done to make her less attractive to other men.'[7] On his way to the front, Agricola encountered one of these women in the custody of a pair of soldiers. 'On my questioning them they explained that the woman had been arrested at the front because of her suspicious conduct in running away. And then with a single movement I snatched the wig from her head. The woman with her shaven head stood trembling in front of us, presenting such a comical spectacle that one of the soldiers laughed so much that he dropped his rifle. Examining the inside of the wig I found some

stitches. These I cut with my penknife – and out fell a message, containing full and accurate details of the advance of our 20th Army Corps' (*AB*, 92).

Swiss mountaineers' hats were sometimes used to convey messages. According to Thomas M. Johnson, in one Swiss café near the French border a man hung his traditional green alpine hat on a peg and sat down to enjoy a bowl of food. After a short time another man wearing a similar hat arrived. Hanging his hat on the peg next to that of the first man, he sat down at a table to order food. Interrupting the first man, he politely asked directions to house number 15. The reply was 'certainly, number 15 is very near you.' The first man finished his lunch and, picking up a hat – the hat of the other man – left the café. Inside the quill of the hat's jaunty feather was a tightly rolled piece of thin paper bearing a secret message (*TJ*, pp 134–5).

Hair, clothing and personal effects such as watches and walking sticks were not the only places in which a person could conceal a message. More intimate parts of the body were also used. Henry Landau claimed that it was not unknown for Belgian refugee women and children to arrive in neutral countries carrying messages secreted in suppository capsules that were, in turn, secreted in their bodies. By 1916, passport privileges for these refugees were withdrawn, and those permitted to leave were always subjected to a body search by German border police (*HL* 1, 81).

Johnson reported the myriad other places in which spies hid their messages: 'in hollow and false teeth, in shoe heels, in the plaster casing of a broken arm, in cotton wound dressings, false curls, garters, and smelling salts. One woman used as hiding-place a baby's intimate draperies. Others were wigs, coat collars, neckties, toothbrush handles, between safety razor blades, in candy, in lead pencils, even in common string. Some messengers carried reports in a pipeful of tobacco.

If caught, they lighted the pipe' (*TJ*, 140). Being able to destroy messages at the last minute was sometimes imperative. Captain Tuohy mentions that it was not uncommon for Belgian refugees to hide reports in bread or other items of food. In an emergency they could quickly make a sandwich of the incriminating pieces of paper (*FT*, 169).

However, swallowing a secret message was not always the end of the story. Agricola encountered a suspected Polish spy who was believed to have swallowed secret information immediately before his capture. Agricola immediately took action to recover the message. 'I now rang up a staff surgeon who was well known to me, and briefly recounted the circumstances. All right, was his answer, I'll send you at once by my servant such powerful purgatives and emetics that in twenty minutes at the latest you'll have the *corpus delicti* – that I'll answer for!' Armed with these powerful emetics, Agricola made his way to the cellar, where the prisoner sat, bound hand and foot, guarded by a military policeman. 'I took the latter aside and asked him, in a whisper, whether the fellow had swallowed anything. "Yes," was the reply; "there's no doubt about that."' Agricola then turned to the spy, telling him that he must take the medicines or he would be compelled to do so by force. The Pole drank the liquid and a result was duly obtained. 'The staff surgeon had not exaggerated,' he reported. 'The medicines certainly were powerful. Ten minutes later the military policeman came to me and laid on the table a small aluminium capsule. As we opened it a tiny slip of paper fell out. It bore a stamp and read as follows: H.Q. 4th Army, Espionage Division. This was the usual credential given to agents to facilitate their passage through the Russian front' (*AB*, 50–52).

Messages could also be concealed in cigars, as Nicholas Everitt discovered while on assignment in Norway in December 1914. Arriving in the fjords for some rest and relaxation after an earlier mission, he was greeted by a Scandinavian friend – 'one of those open-hearted, unsuspecting innocents who led the simple life and believed ill of no man' – who offered him a package. The friend was not perhaps as innocent as he appeared. 'In murmuring my thanks for the parcel, I hazarded the supposition that it probably contained some long-sought smokes. On opening it before his eyes, so to speak, there was disclosed a tin of pipe tobacco and a bundle of cigars, which were at once sampled.' Everitt noticed, however, that one of the cigars – which neither man touched – had its smoking end bitten off, 'having already been tested in a stranger's mouth'. After some smoking and small talk, he took his tobacco away with him to where he could inspect it more closely. 'A careful dissection of the bitten cigar, in the seclusion of my own quarters, brought to light a scrap of paper. A pocket glass helped me to decipher the mystic signs, the interpretation whereof read as follows: "Karl Von S—, a German Artillery officer, married to a native of Scandinavia, is posing as a convalescent consumptive and has been some time in a private villa on the Island of —. He is much too friendly with the wireless operator there, also the garrison officers. Advisable that he be removed at once. You must do it. Act promptly"' (*NE*, 110).

Cigars were used by German agents during the war in a quite different way. A chief in the German intelligence service, Major von Lauenstein, used as one of his aliases 'Mynheer van der Brock', an Amsterdam cigar merchant. He and his agents used cigars not to hide documents but rather to constitute a secret code. Two German naval officers posed as cigar merchants from Holland visiting principal English ports to sell their products. They were equipped with an illustrated catalogue of their wares, whose five sizes were ciphers for naval vessels: very large (battleship), large (battle cruiser), medium (cruiser and light cruiser), small (destroyer and torpedo boat), and very small (submarine). A typical 'order' to their office in Holland ran: 'Harwich: Please send twelve hundred No. 2 Havanas, six hundred No. 3 ditto and two thousand half Coronas.' This meant that there were presently in the harbour twelve battle cruisers, six cruisers and light cruisers, and twenty submarines (*FT*, 166–7).

Other spies were inventive, if perhaps overly dramatic, in hiding documents. Agricola described how a 'suspicious character' was apprehended near the front lines and brought before him for interrogation. 'He reeked of iodoform and claimed to be suffering from venereal disease. As he gave contradictory replies to my questions I ordered his bandages to be removed. Thereupon he began to shriek and struggle, so that we had to bind him. When the bandage was unrolled a message fell out' (*AB*, 92).

Invisible ink was, of course, one of the most traditional ways of concealing information. Captain Tuohy reported that in the early days of the war a Belgian refugee arrived in England carrying a pair of boots wrapped in a copy of the *Étoile Belge* from August 1914. What caught the attention of the officials was that the newspaper – the centre of which had been burned away – was covered in a buttery grease. On closer inspection, they discovered that a message had been inscribed across the grease in invisible lemon–formalin ink, carefully avoiding the burnt hole. The composer of the message had hidden in a ditch and recorded details of all German troop trains that passed through Liège up to 22 August 1914 (*FT*, 170).

In the early days of the war, the Germans used a number of simple methods for sending invisible messages. Writing done in lemon juice could be revealed by ironing the paper with a hot flat iron. Messages inscribed in saliva would appear when the paper was covered with ink, while those written in diluted milk required a dusting of graphite powder. Edwin Woodhall's account of the chemical compositions of various invisible inks used during the war suggests that the Allies ultimately moved well beyond saliva and lemon juice: 'Solution of sugar of lead, in pure water, leaves no trace of writing when dry; but when heated, the written characters turn black. Nitrate of copper, by the same process – red. Nitrate of nickel, by the same process – green. Bromide of copper is very much favoured as it appears promptly by heating, and disappears again when cool. Rice water is invisible, but by the application of iodine stand up blue. Sulphuric acid, or vitriol mixed with water, and the characters written with a fine pointed steel nib makes excellent "invisible ink" as when heated it becomes indelibly black. A feather, with the juice of an onion or turnip, has also been used to write invisible messages, heat application making the characters stand out brown' (*EW*, 146). According to Captain Ferdinand Tuohy, after months of experimenting, British Intelligence developed a red fluid that, when applied to a concealed message, would reveal its contents. The mixture could then be washed off without damaging the message and the report could be sent on without the sender's knowledge (*FT*, 29).

It was obviously important that censorship departments kept up with the increasingly ingenious methods being devised. Agricola reported on the difficulties associated with invisible ink, the possession of which proclaimed the owner as a spy. 'The most difficult part of the matter was the delivery of the ink. If one of these messengers were caught with such ink in his possession he was, of course, a doomed man. There was, too, the further danger that to save his life he might betray those to whom the ink was consigned. The messenger, therefore, had to be both a very astute and an entirely trustworthy person. When writing with invisible ink it was of the first importance to use the softest possible pen, in order to avoid indentations in the paper. A paper which showed scoring between the lines or on the margin was, of course, at once an object of suspicion. And generally the suspicion was well grounded. Such letters or newspapers were naturally placed in a photographic bath without delay' (*AB*, 90–91).

Both Henry Landau and Captain Tuohy report a clever trick devised by German Intelligence to deliver quantities of invisible ink. They first soaked garments, such as socks, vests and handkerchiefs, in chemicals. These garments were then either worn or packed in a suitcase carried by a businessman travelling from a neutral country. Once in England, the clothes would be handed over to the resident German agent, who in turn would soak the clothes to reveal the invisible ink that leaked into the water. The liquid could then be used to write invisible letters. Johnson reported a similar ruse. Female spies wore stockings soaked in a colourless liquid. When the stockings were soaked in warm water, the invisible ink oozed out to be used at a later date. Once the British became aware of this cunning plan, a special analytical laboratory – a kind of forensic laundrette – was established in London to test the clothes and belongings of all suspects arriving from the Continent (*FT*, 171; *HL* 1, 160; *TJ*, 146).

The Germans also gave their spies special inks to be carried in medicines or perfumes, often with a doctor's or dentist's label to avoid suspicion. If caught, a spy could always drink the mixture as it was colourless and harmless. When this ruse was discovered, the Germans began concealing their ink by means of soluble cough drops. In time the Allies confiscated all toilet articles and liquids of anyone crossing frontiers, and also drained their fountain pens (*TJ*,146). But the intelligence chiefs were ever resourceful. According to Johnson, spies sometimes wrote messages on their skin in invisible ink, which the receiver could develop by spreading a special solution over the relevant part of the carrier's body, at which point the message bloomed on the agent's skin (*TJ*, 146).

Invisible ink was far from the only means of conveying information. Codes and ciphers were frequently used by agents, by means of which innocent and everyday objects or actions were turned into carriers of secret meaning. Captain Ferdinand Tuohy warned that even the most harmless looking letters could contain coded messages. As a result, vast numbers of letters were opened during the war. Opening letters closed with wax seals without detection by the recipient would seem a difficult task. However, according to Miklós Soltész, this feat was possible. First, the wax seal was photographed so that it could be repaired exactly as the original. A cut was then made across the wax with a very fine, sharp, hot instrument. The censors had to take the utmost care as sometimes the letters were planted with powder marks, or paper purposely pasted to the interior of the envelope. Occasionally a barely visible thread of silk or a hair was tied to the envelope, to warn the recipient if it had been tampered with. With skill and perseverance, however, the letters could be replaced in their original state (*NS*, 126).

British Intelligence agents, in the course of opening letters written in London and destined for the Continent, uncovered a series of messages passed by a German mother and her daughter. The pair, based in London, wrote enthusiastic letters to a friend in Holland giving – so it appeared – 'enthusiastic accounts of bird life' on Hampstead Heath. 'Eventually the censorship authorities came to the legitimate conclusion that bird life at Hampstead could hardly be of absorbing interest to people living in Holland, whither the letters were addressed, and a comparison of the letters with subsequent raids led to this perfectly legitimate conclusion crystallizing into suspicion and later, into certainty, that the women were spies.' The authorities eventually discovered that these bird-watchers always dispatched their letters after a Zeppelin raid on London. They were arrested and imprisoned (*FT*, 160).

What could appear more innocent than a knitted jumper? However, as Nicholas Everitt discovered, even an object as homely as this could be use to transmit secret messages. 'A parcel sent to a supposed prisoner in a German internment camp', he wrote, 'was found to contain, amongst other things, a woollen sweater, or knitted sports vest. It was apparently so badly knitted, and the wool was seen to be so full of knots, that the censor's suspicions were aroused. Subsequent searches revealed that no such person as the addressee of the parcel in question was known to exist. His name certainly did not appear in any Army List. The aforesaid garment was most carefully unravelled. The wool was found to be whole, with a multitude of simple knots tied at irregular intervals. Alphabets were written on a board, each letter being placed at given distances apart, and very soon a most interesting message was read off' (*NE*, 94).

Placing advertisements in newspapers was common practice, and a special branch of censorship was dedicated to their scrutiny. On one occasion censors kept track of a person who regularly inserted apparently innocuous advertisements in all the English national and provincial newspapers. He would then purchase the papers in which these advertisements appeared, circle them in pencil, and openly forward the newspapers to Holland. On another occasion, according to Captain Tuohy, a particular advertisement in *The Times* 'relative to the sale of a dog was found to conceal the information that a British Division was moving from Salonica to Egypt'.

As well as in advertisements, messages were found to be concealed in the 'agony' column of *The Times*. So that too, Captain Tuohy reported, was 'closely scrutinised lest some seemingly harmless

personal announcement should conceal a code'
(*FT*, 31, 167). Johnson reported that English newspapers were forbidden to publish lottery numbers,
chess games or stamp data in case they contained
hidden messages (*TJ*, 152). Even news stories themselves came under suspicion. War correspondents
were supposed to report the war without bias.
However, Captain Tuohy believed it would be very
easy for certain messages to be hidden in cabled
despatches: 'Thus, the phrase, "The Russians
fought splendidly," might easily be the code for
"The Russians are running out of heavy ammunition"' (*FT*. p. 160). One imagines Captain Tuohy,
in his zest for ferreting out such messages in his
daily papers, becoming like the decipherers in the
kingdom of Tribnia that Jonathan Swift describes
in *Gulliver's Travels*. These individuals are so 'dex-
terous in finding out the mysterious meanings of
words', reports Gulliver, that they can turn the
most banal sentence – 'Our brother Tom has just
got the piles' – into a call to action: 'Resist–, a plot
is brought home – The tour.'[8]

Agricola discovered another way in which a
newspaper could be used by a spy. In June 1915,
he became suspicious of a young man claiming
to be a refugee from Warsaw who was mixing

with German troops in a Polish hamlet. This man had been arrested three times but nothing had ever been found on him. Speaking to him in Russian rather than German, Agricola told him to empty his pockets. These contained a comb, a pair of scissors, a lead pencil and a newspaper. Agricola unfolded the newspaper and held it up to the light. 'I showed the puzzled Town Mayor the tiny, scarcely visible pin-pricks below many of the letters in the newspaper. Then I read him the message thus conveyed' (*AB*, 21).

German agents also concealed messages in parcels containing coded reports worked into the stitching of garments or other cloth articles, using long or short stitches. According to Henry Landau, sometimes parcels wrapped in coloured paper or of a particular shape had a meaning for the recipient. For this reason, the British would delay delivery of parcels, letters and telegrams as long as possible so that any messages sent became worthless for military or naval use (*HL* 1, 160). Sometimes the packaging hid other secrets, since Agricola reported that early in the war secret messages might be concealed under postage stamps: 'There was sufficient space under three or four stamps to write something, though not enough.

Only two or three times did I employ this method of communication' (*AB*, 91).

Coded messages and other pieces of information were conveyed in a bewildering number of ways during the war: in river barges, in balloons, in puffs of smoke, even in dead fish. Landau reported that Belgian *bateliers*, or bargees, regularly concealed messages on their barges when carrying flour and food for the American and Dutch relief organizations. They travelled extensively along the canals in Belgium, sometimes crossing over into occupied France (*HL* 1, 80). Other messages were sent aloft in the baskets of small balloons, which drifted across the front until the Germans shot them down and retrieved the messages. Orders were soon issued by the British that any balloons spotted should be shot down immediately to prevent them from crossing the lines (*FT*, 134). One Allied agent decided to shoot messages across the high-voltage electrified fence along the Belgian–Dutch border using a bow and arrows. However, after four or five messages had been successfully retrieved, the agent was apprehended by the Germans (*HL* 1, 81). Other efforts at breaching this electrified fence involved merely throwing reports across, to be retrieved by local farm labourers (*HL* 1, 80).

Carrier and homing pigeons had been used in warfare since the middle of the nineteenth century. When it became evident that the Germans were using them for communication purposes, the order came down from the British authorities that all of them should be shot on sight. To help one of their pigeons escape the Allied firing squad, the Germans dyed it green and red, disguising it as a parrot. Unfortunately, the bird was unable to escape the daily massacre (*FT*, 137).

These birds needed to be delivered into enemy territory so that they could carry information from agents back home. Edwin Woodhall described a close call experienced by a French soldier delegated to conveying a pair of pigeons into German territory. The soldier, dressed as a peasant, was dropped near Mézières, on the Franco–Belgian border. He wore a waistcoat with deep pockets in which to carry the pigeons, Pauline and Victor. He showed his papers to the two guards, who waved him through the checkpoint. After a few steps, however, Pauline began cooing so the spy was forced to have a coughing and sneezing fit to hide the sounds. Luckily, the birds escaped notice, and on the following day they were released into the air with the information around their legs.

Woodhall was later sentimental about Pauline: 'She was, oh, so lovable! But like all the ladies, dangerous!' (*EW*, 89–90).

Pigeons were not the only creatures used to convey messages. Woodhall described how reports reached the Allies that soldiers in the trenches had seen a dog 'suddenly appear from, or go into the enemy lines, generally just before dawn'. The dog – soon nicknamed Fritz – was suspected by the Allies of being used as a runner, slipping between the lines with messages. For weeks on end he was seen going about his business, but the Allies were unable to catch him. 'What its mission was, and where it went to, behind our lines, nobody could tell', Woodhall reported. 'We set a watch to trap this dog, but strict orders were issued that he was to be taken alive, and for this purpose a little mongrel bitch name "Rosie" was called into service.' It was a classic honeytrap. Fritz was duly caught – and he had a message attached to his collar with instructions for a spy to obtain coordinates of Allied troop movements. Fortunately for Fritz he was not shot at dawn. '"Fritz" was adopted by a battery nearby, where, with "Rosie" he became the mascot and pet of the gunners. Later, during the "strafing" of this battery by the German guns,

"Fritz" was killed' (*EW*, 150). Concerns that other dogs were being used as carriers to communicate messages across the lines meant that in Arras in 1917 an Allied intelligence officer was given the task of tracking local dogs. All dogs straying near the line were ordered to be shot (*FT*, 138–9).

Even dead fish were suspected of transporting messages for the Germans. At Arras, where the River Scarpe flowed east towards the German lines, the Allies became concerned that dead fish were being used to carry communications in their bellies. 'What simpler', asked Tuohy, 'than for a piscatorial spy to catch a fish, cut it open, insert his report, and then throw deceased back into the river?' To foil the plot, three huge nets were spread daily across the Scarpe to catch anything hidden in the river. It was the unenviable task of several intelligence officers to pick through the debris every day, looking for piscatorial spies (*FT*, 139).

Other ingenious methods of communication were developed, and so prolific were they that the entire Western Front, from its windmills to its laundry lines, must have seemed charged with secret meanings. For example, the arms of windmills were operated by the Germans using the Morse code dot-and-dash principle. When British Intelligence realized what was happening, most civilians living near the windmills were evacuated and the activity of the windmills closely observed. It soon became clear which ones were being used to send messages (*FT*, 135–6).

Clocks in public places were also suspected. Since the town hall clock in Ypres was always wrong, rumours spread on both sides that it was being manipulated in order to send messages. However, the Germans, either through suspicion or by accident, shelled the town hall – so no longer did it tell the right or wrong time, let alone send messages (*FT*, 135).

Farmers and their labourers were suspected of aiding the espionage effort. According to Captain Tuohy, one Royal Flying Corps officer advised British Intelligence that it was possible for someone to signal information to a German pilot by ploughing a field in a particular way. For example, not to plough a field could mean 'all quiet in this sector' or ploughing in 'tiger stripes' might indicate that the British were preparing to attack locally. 'So started a ploughed field scare', wrote Captain Tuohy. Intelligence ordered the Royal Flying Corps to make a complete photographic survey of the rear of British lines. These prints were pasted into a consecutive whole, after which the 'panorama of fields and woods and roads was then minutely studied through a magnifying glass like a magic lantern apparatus, lest any peculiarities in local ploughing had developed.' When a discrepancy arose, an intelligence officer was despatched to question the peasant farmer, who often looked on in total bemusement (*FT*, 134–5).

On rivers and at sea, the most harmless sights were sometimes laden with secret meanings. Kaledin reported that German fishermen used different-coloured sails on their boats to send messages in a kind of special semaphore (*VK*, 62). At Vlamertinghe in Belgium, a nun would signal to German gunners by emitting puffs of smoke from her chimney whenever British troops were passing through the village (*FT*, 133–4).

Even laundry, according to some reports, was used by the Germans. According to Captain Tuohy, the British could not understand why women remained in the shelled and broken hamlets in the Ypres Salient where, to earn a living, they had to carry out laundry work for the troops. Rumours began to circulate that these women were signalling to the enemy by spreading out their washing to dry in particular shapes. It became evident that one day a field would be drying a vast circle of shirts, on another day a huge cross of trousers. When a 28 cm shell landed in the centre of a battalion of the Monmouthshire Regiment as they marched along the Brielen road, killing or wounding the entire unit, the women were blamed. Captain Tuohy was ordered to watch them, his watch extending into the night where he lay in the cold and damp, looking for a sign that they were using lamps or fires to communicate messages. He could discover no evidence against them, however (*FT*, 136–7).

Establishments such as brothels and public buildings were venues where information could be passed, sometimes through nonverbal means such as tapping. A German spy was able to send messages to the double agent Victor Kaledin in the wine cellars of the brothels around the railway and ports. The spy applied a light coating of grease to the wall and tapped a message. The message would be picked up by the person in the adjoining room, who then – in a kind of cellar telegraph – repeated the process until it passed through each cellar before reaching its destination, always a private house facing the sea (*VK*, 62).

Kaledin encountered this kind of coded finger-tapping on another occasion, this time in a slum hotel in the district of Ochta, a suburb of St Petersburg. His disguise on this occasion was Colonel Nicholas Mousin, a 'drink-sodden creature, cashiered from an obscure line regiment on a charge of gambling and petty theft'. One night as he sat huddled by his fire in his room he heard a tapping at his door. When he opened it, a 'woman of exceptional beauty' came inside. 'I bowed, but she did not speak, and she not so much evaded my scrutiny as paid no attention to me at all.' After sitting in a chair and lighting a cigarette, she began tapping her fingers sharply on the arm of the chair. 'German messenger code! My pulse beat a trifle faster, and presently the ghost of a smile twitched my lips.' The woman was imparting a message from Major von Lauenstein that Kaledin was to get himself into the hospital at Tzarskoe-Selo, where he would have his rendezvous with the dying Abraam Portnoy (*VK*, 23–6).

9

Loose lips:
gossips and counterspies

THE CAPTION from the famous World War II
poster – 'Loose Lips Might Sink Ships' – was
equally relevant in World War I. Keeping information secret obsessed Captain Ferdinand Tuohy.
He worried about what he called 'vanity-babble'
from 'the talkative naval officer's wife' who might
say too much over cocktails and canapés (*FT*, 59).
He was also particularly concerned about the
trustworthiness of European aristocrats with their
intermarriages across borders. Any princess on the
throne of a foreign country, however ineffectual
she appeared, could be a potential agent. She had
access to Cabinet documents and Cabinet councils,
she attended important dinner parties and ban-
quets where she was ideally placed to pick up any
gossip – such as the 'vanity-babble' of the naval
wife – that might be let slip. Having learnt the

inner secrets of state, she would be able to report back to her native land, and on occasion to take orders from her own family that could influence policy in her adopted home (*FT*, 75).

Nicholas Everitt was suspicious of officials at British consulates abroad. 'We in the Secret Service had been impressively warned before leaving England to avoid our Ambassadors abroad as we would disciples of the devil' (*NE*, 240). He pointed out that in 1914 more than thirty British consuls posted abroad bore German names, indicating a vast system of infiltration. 'Glance through the following astounding list. In Sweden, twenty-four out of thirty-one British Consuls and Vice-Consuls are non-Englishmen; in Norway, twenty-six out of thirty; in Denmark, nineteen out of twenty-six; in Holland and its Colonies, fourteen out of twenty-four; in Switzerland nine out of fourteen.' He noted that the few consuls who were actually Englishmen were generally posted at places with ski resorts (*NE*, 249).

Threats to national security did not merely come from the top of society. Captain Tuohy also warned about *vivandières*, the female camp followers, or sutlers, who attached themselves to regiments, selling provisions and liquor. He thought that only France could have produced such women: simple peasant girls, attracted by the whirlwind of war and prospect of adventure, with no shortage of officer admirers with whom to share a bottle of champagne. Most of these women were innocent enough, though some eavesdropped and needed to be kept under observation as potential spies (*FT*, 101).

In the spring of 1915, Edwin Woodhall was charged with observing a suspected spy, a wine merchant who plied his trade at Hazebrouck, near

France's border with Belgium. He raised suspicions because, as Woodhall noted, 'the amount of business he transacted was … not nearly so interesting as the concern he displayed in our military dispositions all along the route of his journey.' As the merchant made his way through the countryside in a pony and trap, Woodhall followed him on his Triumph motorcycle. 'My first trip behind this seemingly harmless "wine merchant" was to the little village of Nerf Berquin, at that period a highly important spot, as it contained a huge concentration of mechanical tractors and heavy guns; in other words it was an artillery park of our very latest armament.' One day Woodhall shadowed him as he made deliveries on the road to Armentières. 'In one spot I saw him halt his pony, as though resting it, near one of our large aviation aerodromes. He evidently did a good deal of memorizing and if the facts he ascertained were only possible of secret transmission they must have been first-class information for his German paymasters in Holland' (*FT*, 246–7). Woodhall recommended that the merchant be arrested, but because his papers were in order and his cases of wine dutifully delivered, and because he memorized his facts and wrote nothing down, no action was taken.

There was always a danger of vital information leaking out. Seemingly innocent gossip by men coming ashore could be collated by trained spies who were always hanging around the docks. The problem was particularly intense in Salonica (present-day Thessaloniki) in Greece, where spies from every part of the world competed for information. The Allied headquarters was located right in the centre of the city. 'Go anywhere at Salonica,' wrote Captain Tuohy, 'to Floca's bar or to the White Tower restaurant, and one overheard officers and staff officers talking shop – intimate local shop – in their various tongues.' It was perfectly possible for a trained ear to pick up the gossip of these officers. The problem was how to keep the local population separate. A French general, according to Tuohy, hit upon a clever expedient: 'General Sarrail, in a typically Gallic way, made an effort to stop such leakage of information by importing from Paris and Marseilles about fifty women known to the police, the idea being to keep officers at Salonica apart from the civilian population.' Civilian labour was banned from Allied Officers clubs and only French staff, such as waiters imported from France, were hired (*FT*, 59, 121).

Talkative civilians were not the only potential loose lips. The counterspy is a member of the Intelligence Service whose job is to watch not only foreign agents but also his own spies, in case one of them is a double agent. According to Captain Tuohy, it is the most difficult job in espionage, 'deceiving people whose own job in life is to deceive' (*FT*, 37).

Every platoon in the AEF (American Expeditionary Forces) included at least one 'Silent

Watcher' who secretly kept tabs on about sixty men. Only one person, his senior officer, would know of his role; this officer would receive the weekly reports, which he would pass on until they eventually came to rest at G-2-B at Chaumont, the AEF headquarters. Silent Watchers had only one purpose and that was to detect spying and disloyalty. Their brief did not extend to reporting violations of regulations, lax morals or even crime (*TJ*, 104). In each area where American troops were stationed, one or more counter-espionage officers, assisted by between three and twenty-four Intelligence Police, were employed directly by G-2-B. They travelled widely on motorcycles under various pretexts, wearing uniform, civilian clothes or camouflage (*TJ*, 108). The Corps of Intelligence Police (IP) did the legwork for the counterspies, searching for German spies in areas which the Silent Watchers were not able to cover, such as among the civilian populations of England, France, Belgium and, later, Germany itself and Luxembourg (*TJ*, 107).

There were a number of successful double agents – men or women who spied for two masters, playing one off against the other. Victor Kaledin spied for both the Russians and the Germans. To the Russians he was known as agent K.14, and to the Germans as O.M.66. He defined a double spy as a highly trained agent introduced deliberately into the Secret Service of a foreign power. Such a spy bears a huge responsibility, often having to become judge, jury and executioner all in one day, and possibly sacrificing his own countryman in order to save a whole battalion. A double spy, therefore, had to be mentally strong enough to accept sacrificing the few in order to save the many. And always his own life hung by a thread. If detected he stood completely alone. The official story would be that he defied orders and took action into his own hands – in other words, he went AWOL. A clerk would destroy his papers, his name would be forgotten, and no recognition would be given for his work. The double spy, therefore, performed his tasks purely out of love and loyalty for his country. Kaledin made an appeal: 'The double spy deserves surely a measure, at least, of human sympathy and understanding' (*VK*, 17).

Glossary

AEF American Expeditionary Forces.

AGRICOLA Code name for Alexander Bauermeister.

CIRCULAR CODE A system of double flats (short pauses) in between guide words.

CONTRE-SPY Secret Service spies who watch their own agents. Also known as counter-spies.

DEAD LETTER A defective shell.

DETECTASCOPE A small globular, fish-eye lens that could be inserted in small spaces, allowing the operator to see into a room.

DISTANT AGENTS Agents who have their base of operations far into the enemy's interior.

DOUBLE AGENT A highly trained agent deliberately introduced into the Secret Service of a foreign power.

FOOL-SPY A spy unaware that he or she is being used as a decoy in order to protect the identity of a more important spy.

G-2 American Intelligence HQ attached to the American Expeditionary Forces based at Chaumont-sur-Aire in provincial Lorraine.

HQ Headquarters.

ILLUMINATES Women who make friends with the target's wife or girlfriend in order to ferret out information that could be used against the target.

INTERLOCKING CODE Two meaningless words giving the correct letters of the actual word used in the original message.

IP The Corps of Intelligence Police doing the legwork for the counter-spies.

'ITOK' OR 'IT' A listening device planted in no-man's-land to hear the enemy's conversations.

JIM Code name for Nicholas Everitt.

K.14 Russian code name for Russian double agent Victor Kaledin.

KRENDL Pretzel-shaped sweet yeast bread filled with dried fruits.

LETTER-BOX Resident agent to whom reports were delivered.

MORSE CODE A code in which letters are represented by various combination of two signs – e.g. dot and dash, long and short flash, etc.

PACKING Russian term used when the streets are filled with agents in disguise.

POW Prisoner of war.

PROMENEURS Agents who moved from village to village collecting information.

O.M.66 German code name for Russian double-agent Victor Kaledin.

SILENT WATCHERS Agents employed to detect spying and disloyalty within an American platoon.

SOUND RANGING The determination of position by timing arrival of sounds from known points.

STOOL PIGEON A spy deliberately placed with prisoners in order to direct conversation to reveal information.

STRAFING Bombardment with shells, bombs or sniper fire.

STUNTING An act or performance to scare prisoners into revealing information.

T.43 Code name for Miklós Soltész (pen name Nicholas Snowden).

VIVANDIÈRES Female camp followers who attached themselves to regiments, selling provisions and liquor.

Notes and references

ABBREVIATIONS

AB Lieutenant Alexander Bauermeister, *Spies Break Through: Memoirs of a German Secret Service Officer* (London: Constable, 1934).

EW Edwin T. Woodhall, *Spies of the Great War: Adventures with the Allied Secret Service* (London: John Long, 1932).

FT Captain Ferdinand Tuohy, *The Secret Corps: A Tale of 'Intelligence' on all Fronts* (London: John Murray, 1920).

HL1 Henry Landau, *All's Fair: The Story of the British Secret Service behind German Lines* (New York: G.P. Putnam's Sons, 1934).

HL2 Henry Landau, *Spreading the Spy Net: The Story of a British Spy Director* (London: Jarrolds, 1938).

NE Nicholas Everitt, *British Secret Service During the Great War* (London: Hutchinson, 1920)

NS Nicholas Snowden, *Memoirs* of a Spy (London: Jarrolds, 1934).

TJ Thomas Marvin Johnson, *Secret War: Espionage and Counter-espionage* (London: Jarrolds, 1930).

VK Colonel Victor K. Kaledin, *K.14.–O.M.66: Adventures of a Double Spy* (London: Hurst & Blackett, 1934).